T0038221

Dayo

Dayo

Marc Perez

Brick Books

Library and Archives Canada Cataloguing in Publication

Title: Dayo / Marc Perez.
Names: Perez, Marc, author.
Identifiers: Canadiana (print) 20230583520 | Canadiana (ebook) 20230583539 |
ISBN 9781771316286 (softcover) | ISBN 9781771316293 (EPUB) |
ISBN 9781771316309 (PDF)
Subjects: LCGFT: Poetry.
Classification: LCC PS8631.E73333 D39 2024 | DDC C811/.6—dc23

We gratefully acknowledge the Canada Council for the Arts, the Government of
Canada through the Canada Book Fund, and the Ontario Arts Council and the
Government of Ontario for their support of our publishing program.

Edited by Cara-Lyn Morgan.
Author photo by Marc Perez.
The book is set in Kepler Std.
Design by Marijke Friesen.

Brick Books
487 King St. W.
Kingston, ON
K7L 2X7
www.brickbooks.ca

Though much of the work of Brick Books takes place on the ancestral lands of the
Anishinaabeg, Haudenosaunee, Huron-Wendat, and Mississaugas of the Credit
peoples, our editors, authors, and readers from many backgrounds are situated
from coast to coast to coast in Canada on the traditional and unceded territories of
over six hundred nations who have cared for Turtle Island from time immemorial.
While living and working on these lands, we are committed to hearing and
returning the rightful imaginative space to the poetries, songs, and stories that
have been untold, under-told, wrongly told, and suppressed through colonization.

para sa mga dayo

CONTENTS

I.   BUTÓ

Suddenly I realize
That if I stepped out of my body I would break
Into blossom.
> —James Wright

FORM AS A LIVING THING

The aratilis grows in the empty lots of demolished homes. It thrives
often where the toilet used to be. Form is the act of blossoming
in unlikely vessels. *displacement and immobility*. Omniscience
from confinement. If not a writer, then a tree. A planter or a pruner.
A harvester or an indoor cactus admirer. Absorb and release, breathe.
Spread like moss in gutters. *bodies out of place.* Form is the leaf
that sprouts from your toes. The scent of grass in your hair.

BONES ARE SEEDS

But now the stark dignity of
entrance—Still, the profound change
has come upon them: rooted, they
grip down and begin to awaken
   —William Carlos Williams

The island greets me with satin
clouds and light rain, parting
as the ferry docks at the cove.
Rough as the precipice, my mind
careens to the chimes of a concertina—
and my heart begins to grieve,
Here he is, the man without
love, country or soul—forgotten,
abandoned, buried with no tomb.
But now the stark dignity of

remembrance. Tracing the ebb
of history, I turn each pebble
and seashell, washed in time
and polished with seaside
reflections: *Your breath is home,*
a shelter amidst the plague.
The coastal forest is a testament
to your banished footprints,
a welcoming totem to your life's
entrance—Still, the profound change

arrives in the form of a deer
traversing slopes of wild berries
and fern to bid farewell. For now,
I use the North Shore mountains
as your headstones and the sakura
blossoms for candles, while I pray
and offer a song of loss and rebirth.
My feet, too, are planted in a land
that is not my own, and the tide
has come upon them—uprooted, they

find themselves in hostile shores
like driftwood carried by turbulent
currents. Unable to return, we learn
and adapt to numbing rain and snow.
They do not know where we come from
bones are also seeds—even in barren
landscapes, untended, we flower.
They can cast us in a crevice, nameless,
yet we continue to survive,
grip down and begin to awaken.

WAKING

If it were sufficient to love
we wouldn't wake up each morning to part
curtains, air time's vacancies,

water the potted plants—
prime orchids and succulents,
the Christmas cactus that blooms in summer.

Or keep our thoughts attuned to ordinary sacredness,
like the unfurling of fiddleheads.

And if we lived long enough
for our fertile hands to nourish the soil itself
and the pothos taking root in wells within us;

if it rained even in the most arid of days,
things would be too easy.

MEDITATIONS

i
sargassum purls
blanket the pebble beach
while a pair of kelp stipe
drums on driftwood—
echoes of a coastal kulintang

ii
the river's undercurrent betrays movement—
the rocks & dead salmon appear to have been
where they've always been

iii
as I weave strands
of cedar bark into a rose, pliant
braids of light & dark

memory reveals patterns—
a leaf caught in the eddies of a lagoon

iv
the satin sheen
of wet wood on my fingertips—
I am here, still here

EXTINCTIONS

And now, the end is near. You ask
me to turn off

the radio. Where you're from,
people get shot if they don't karaoke

"My Way" right. You
want quiet. We're here,

you say, tapping
the table's edge,

killing
ourselves,

and for what? Not knowing,
no longer

loving. I remember you
screaming

at the TV when the beluga
from Vancouver

Aquarium was merely shipped
to another tanked life

somewhere in Europe. I reach
for you, but your hand clenches

away, because
it's my fault—not the beluga's

fate, but ours—
and you recite names

of extinct animals until
the list includes you and me.

PLUVIAL: A PARKING LOT PASTORAL

Walking through a Grandview
Highway parking lot, I hear frogs

croak behind a row of cars.
But there are no lilied waters,

patches of moss green amid
fallow fields, nothing

but ditches filled with plastic,
antidepressant residue.

Maybe I'm tired of waiting
for the moon beyond harvest,

mirroring clear skies on mud.
Yes, my heart longs to sing

a kundiman for clean streams
as my shoes slide on opal

oil spill, cornflakes scattering
like bougainvillea blossoms

plucked by an immortal
monsoon. From asphalt,

I praise clouds for reprieve,
rain for another poem.

WHEN THE HEART CATCHES COLD

The counsellor suggests surrounding myself
with fragrant flowers to calm my limbic system.

You'll feel better, she says, *and experience
drastic changes in your mood.* The calligraphy

scroll on her wall reminds me of T'ao Ch'ien,
who left the floating world for gardens and fields

to tend and die in—honeysuckle, wisteria, pine,
and bamboo groves. But there is no Spring

in this city, so I go to a Dollar Store for scents
in plastic bottles. As if lost in a cold mountain mist,

the vapour spreads like a clandestine shroud
in the black-mould-infested basement where I lie

naked and alone beside a leafless banyan bonsai
weaving towards the full moon and bright stars.

SUICIDE ON REPLAY

I.

The six-tatami-mat room leads to Roka's dark wood bungalow
cradled in a tangle of bamboo grove. The narrow engawa creaks as
I enter a shoji. A woodblock calligraphy in kanji offers a greeting:
Farm when it's sunny. Read when it rains. I trace *Footprints in the
Snow* to a carved rock sitting in a forest of green ginkgo.

a sparrow's shadow
rests on my itchy eyelids
glimmer of koi fish

II.

I eat a bowl of tororo soba before embarking into the fluorescent
labyrinth of Sunshine City, where people mirror desires in a
kaleidoscope. I exit in the suburban dimness of Zōshigaya and
locate grave one-fourteen-one-three to recite a solemn dream for
the spirit of Sōseki. Somewhere near a sakura tree, Sensei's friend,
K., is also laid to rest.

a lady wearing
a pink hat lights incense sticks
eulogy in smoke

III.

I walk along a railroad track to search for the footbridge where
Osamu once stood, leaning against a railing, gazing at the sunrise or
sunset. It is hard to tell when things are in black and white. I climb
up the unsteady structure. The massive sun renders the sky scarlet,
blurring tracks that stretch to the horizon as trains slither like
snakes beneath.

nascent autumnal
grass on Tamagawa's berm
suicide on replay

THIS WORLD IS AN AQUARIUM

A two-meter cylinder teeming with moon jelly,
destinies swirling in a measured galaxy
of glass and steel. There's a constellation
of red acne on my chin, mere specks
in a world about to collapse. I don't want
to be asleep in apocalypse. This morning,
on the bus, something sharp scratches
my left cheek. Nobody pauses to notice.
Passengers continue to glide, arms swaying
like tentacles on Pacific's epipelagic zone.
When forests burn down in a heat dome,
atmospheric rivers submerge the suburbs,
lake water reclaiming its bed from concrete.

Everything is saturated,
luminescent blue.

SOLSTICE

snowed in
I watch winter

initiate birth
& in death

sprouts flourishing
I moon for you

to share
a handful of seed

you laugh
knowing I grew up

believing life
begins in spring

A SEED

Under a dogwood, yellow
petals strewn about our feet. Maybe
white? You spoke in aphorisms,
shared a recent daydream about
a dead poet or vagabond—a chance
encounter with Villon, wearing
his funny hat by a riverbank
in Tokyo, holding a poster ad
for skin-whitening facial soap.
You then pointed to a tree across
the pond, said it was pine. That was
when I wondered how you learned
to differentiate conifers, sure that
one is neither spruce nor fir. Without
doubts. A sprig of abandon sprung
from your chest. No, it wasn't faith—
a seed, tossed by a bluebird.

THE POET AS A QUIDNUNC

for Karla & Chris

what now? autumn leaves—
ginkgo & red maple

splayed on a log bench
I peer through stratified light

shadows, fog & bearded boughs
eavesdrop on the whispers

between moss & pebbles
seagulls noshing on dead fish

an eagle on a treetop silo
whorled shrubs in hibernation

the hush of a bamboo thicket
each moment, a theatre

of devised visions   sounds
reach my ears—mumbled

prayers, a chuckle emanating
from the god of gossip

TRANSIT

overcast glimpses
through a skylight gloom

I take the nineteen
bus instead of Sky-
train, not because it moves
seawards, but it passes

the corner of King-
sway & Fraser where
about-to-bloom
yellow magnolia bulbs

guide the day
labourers waiting
on damp grass

like a hundred candelabras

ARS POETICA

To compose a poem is to start fire. I agree. *Now is the time*
for furnaces, and only light should be seen. Provide warmth
to unclothed bodies. To be human is to envision, dream
about voices from the margins of your bed, where bones
are enjambed like a cathedral of firewood. If not combustion,
then a verse on how to reclaim love. Yes, *poetry, like bread,*
is for everyone. Unseen, your red ink shines as stars at noon.
To write words that burn is arson: set your tongue on fire.

A BRIEF HISTORY OF WALLS

It's only in darkness you can see the light,
says Charles in "Looking Around." Listening
to a Vancouver radio station as fascists
rally on the lawn of City Hall, fighting

for their right to be housekeepers and gardeners,
welfare recipients. A war against drugs raging
in Manila has killed more than thirty thousand
poor people. A victim's mother builds a union.

A child dies at a desert border and an old dude
donning a MAGA hat, watching flash news
on a 4K flat screen, blames the boy for believing

walls are permeable. A Japanese man sits cross-
legged at the bottom of a forest well, mumbling,
Only from emptiness that things start to fill.

LOCKED DOWN

couched, attuned
to the chorus

of cicadas
complaining
about pavements

on fire & unplanted

in a heat wave
that kills forty
& those who can afford

to frolic & dream
left in the mountains

to play with the pebbles
of the stream

TO BE A TREE

first you need sunlight
and a handful of earth

dig your feet
deep enough
so that your toes wet a bit

don't worry about water
rain will come
shower you like when you were young
a seedling

branch your arms
and twig your fingers

chase the sunset
until somewhere

or maybe on your shoulder
a swallow

A NOTE

after Wisława Szymborska

death is the only way
to be dressed in fine clothing
bathed in tears
eaten by worms

to spread wings
or to wag a tail

to tell a stone
from a leaf

reduced to ashes
grow into a forest
to return to distant roots

to exist in murmured stories
and bittersweet eulogies
with the casket closed

only if granted a chance
to watch from a pew
keep a memory or two
pack a memento

of being
alive

II.   ARKIPELAGO

Remember: we carry our culture in the canoes of our bodies.
Remember: home is not simply a house, village, or island;
home is an archipelago of belonging.
            —Craig Santos Perez

BODY OF WATER

Home is a place where rivers meet
the sea. Fill my lungs with brackish
delta water. Estero de Tripa de Gallina,
childhood memory's tributary, stagnant
in black silt and methane—only the dead
remember your lilies. But this is no longer
about drowning. I've outgrown my fear
of letting go. This is surrender, a body
defying buoyancy—sunken and supine
on the seabed like the sedimented hull
of a capsized ship. Reel in my feet
from a cerulean reef, swathed in seaweed.
There's room for you here—a soft bed
among corals. Come, I'll breathe you in.

AUBADE, AN AIRPORT & THE SEAS

I reach for you
as though for the mugicha

we drank
at a seashore
teahouse in Kamakura

while you sit
on a metal bench

losing your voice
in separate

spaces   with a brown hand
a border agent tugs

the pen holder with a tarsier
perched on a palm tree
from your suitcase

didn't you know
you're not allowed

unaware
I bought it for you in Bohol
on a low tide sandbar

where we tasted salty sea
urchins from spiny shells

cracked in half

by a sunned boy
who seemed to emerge
straight from the sea

reminding you of a folktale
about a young fisherman & a sea turtle

as fractures mature us

I wish for waves
to come

come
crashing at the airport
to submerge & claim us   another

border

agent who could have been
your sister tells us you need to leave

that you have no right
to be here   go back

to the land of daybreak

across the seas
where we were born
without me

BASUE

*... a certain depressed aesthetic and melancholia of a social place, such as
a dingy bar, a rundown motel or a dirty eatery where the poor gather and secret
lovers meet, hiding from the bright city lights and the noise of modern prosperity.*
—Dai Kojima

The bar smells of wet wood. I lean against cold hardness. The wallpaper
peels. Master hovers behind an opaque vitrine, a discordant display

of bare flesh. The whiskey percolates in my mouth, less bitter
than the dredged vignettes in my head. I adjust my wristwatch and glance

at the clock, time hemmed in by two black-and-white posters of sumo
wrestlers, the creases on their naked bodies like lubricated pieces

of a somatic puzzle, clashing tectonic plates dreaming to form a mountain.
The door opens. A siren sounds in the distance. I look over my shoulder

as if expecting a friend, a lover, familiar face of a stranger. There's no one
I know except for the humid breeze. The incandescent bulbs overhead

reluctantly dim. I scribble a name on the amber bottle with a felt pen
and pass it on to the ponytailed boy behind me, waiting patiently

for some sort of departure. If you spend enough nights on foreign streets
you begin to embody the anxious intimacies of street lamps and moonlight.

IN MEMORIAM

you listen to the thrum of her chest where you once lay sleeping hoping for it to last & you keep on thinking of the times when she left & came back for you crying on the first day of kindergarten eyes suspiciously glued to her face as she leaned against a mango tree beckoning you to look ahead face the mean blackboard when you got home you found out that your father had taken her to the airport bound for Hong Kong to wipe tables & scrub toilets your elder sisters insisted you now had to wash dishes & iron your school uniform for you no longer had a mother until she came back four years later when her employment contract ended & bribed you out to a casino & abandoned you in the care of cashiers at McDonald's on United Nations Avenue leaving you with a pile of fries & burgers to dream & forget when she had no money left she came home to the place where she had left you so long ago now waiting for you to tell her your name & you listen closely for a heartbeat in her chest where you once lay sleeping & it whispers something but you no longer remember her name

THE NANNY

Your nanny graces my place
around noon, on her break

time from your porticoed
Point Grey mansion.

She flutters noiselessly,
leaving traces of her presence—

scent of roasted coconut shreds
in my gloomy one-bedroom basement,

touches of bleach, detergent crystals,
sparkling oven and countertops,

sweet tea in the fridge and cassava cake,
a steamy pot of rice spiriting away.

On the table, a short note:
Dear Bunso—Love, Nanay.

AUTOBIOGRAPHY: MANILA

... the child's surroundings provide clues to help in orientation.
  —Oxford English Dictionary

A palace abandoned and students in blue
jeans cling on spire gates. My mother,
named after the color of loam, delivers
her son in a ghost-den, while her husband
hauls desert city sand dunes onto ten-
wheelers—Saudi Boy. I smoke weed
before menthols. School is the pipeline
gateway. I sniff glue in ruby. Generator
eardrums, methane water. My jobless teacher
pawns her house to be a housekeeper. Bananas,
copper, people for export—remittances
balikbayan boxes, photographs of someone
else's blue-eyed children. I stash a headless
lighter with aluminum coiled around
a ballpoint cartilage, sip 3-in-1 coffee
for breakfast, methamphetamined
before home economics. Barbed-wire
walls, broken-glass cement. Guards
armed with revolvers. At billiard
halls, I never win against the dude
with eleven fingers. Instead, I roll
the dice, toss three coins, shuffle cards
for lunch—a bald rat chases a kitten

or the chick limp in its mouth—
    A long-distance call: *Come home!*
    I answer. Nobody's home.

CROSSING

I.   borderlands

fleeing from the country
he escaped to
the fields of powder shine
sharper than a tyrant's
machete slashing
fingers and toes
as he wades
through forests
buried in whiteness
trudging slowly
on the faces
of rocks gasping for air
under the shadow
of dead stars
he aims a crystalline fist
at the heavens
taunting the gods
with a bonfire hunger
defiant ember
burning brighter
than the written and unwritten laws
of this and that land

II.   seas

the prime minister apologizes
for lives lost
aboard the MS *St. Louis*
precious
as those on *Komagata Maru*
or the sunburnt migrants
adrift on rubber
boats bloating the Mediterranean
but he has no idea
what it means
to be driven into exile
salvage photographs already saved
from fire
have no room for memories
dock on a shore
and not touch the sand
turned away again
and again left
to be swallowed
by raging tides
of men—
landless
asleep on waves
buried at sea

FILIAL AFFAIRS

I.

When rain and wind
coalesce in a wintry night
isolation's sole consolation
is a sip of warm whiskey

while Kusano's festive
frogs croak drunkenly
on the dreary yellowed
pages of a paperback.

II.

My dear father's bones
different from Nakahara's—

powder in marble
container, locked in closet,
brought out in nostalgia.

III.

Mother flies to Chieko's sky.
Though she haunts no wind,

hears no voice,
and chants no curse,

as her sunken eyes shed tears,
a man-child scribbles verses.

BALIKBAYAN BOX

a box to contain the American dream:
body lotion & hand cream
crunchy peanut butter
Dove & Irish Spring bar soap
enveloped hundred-dollar bill
Fruit of the Loom T-shirts
Gain laundry detergent & softener
Head & Shoulders anti-dandruff shampoo
instant coffee & powdered cream
Jordan 3
Kisses, Toblerone, M&Ms, Musketeers & Mars
Levi's 501
microwave & oven toaster
No Name pasta
Oxford English Dictionary and Thesaurus
PlayStation console
Queen Elizabeth Park in spring, framed
radio & CD player
SPAM, pork & beans, corned beef
Toshiba television
underwear & socks
Vancouver Canucks jersey
wristwatches
Xmas card
Yankees snapback hat
zinc duct-tape

HIGH JUNCTIONS

Jeepneys belch diesel smoke all over San Andres. A bottle
of Do-All sears your nostrils, glues you to the night sky

to hide in its shadows, stash light in your pockets. With loose
change, burn crystal rocks to clamber up and hang yourself

in the crescent moon, buried beneath moonrocks. You know
what work is—pushing a wooden cart, its metal wheels trotting

on tropical alleys, monsoon noondays or eves, harvesting dated
newspapers and bottles, broken things / remember, years ago,

making your way through smog and mist, you chanced upon
a garden where orchids bloomed on the brittle branches

of a caimito tree, its supple fruits dangling like amethyst
pendants over your head. You sheltered in the shade, clasped

a warm cup of sun-dried angel's trumpet, a celestial brew.
Bowed, as if in prayer, before bells that refused to peal.

RUPTURES

at twelve | you vanished on a nameless bus | to a province
where your grandmother danced | with her orchids
until your uncle caught you with | menthols between | your lips
he offered you a meal | before dragging you | to a varnished bench
reprimanded | with a leather belt | by your father | who feared
he had lost | another son | *don't do drugs* | *don't get stabbed* | awoken
by cries that echoed like vespers | on the street | where you used to
play | running | now to your aunt | hunched on a pavement | in a crowd
men lifted your dead | uncle by his legs & armpits | his torso
slipping from strained | stained hands | flesh scraping the asphalt
like the lump of meat | you once saw | dangling on a hook at Paco
Market | where air felt heavy as mud | a hole dotted the tall
ridge of his nose | & trails oozed out from the back | of his head
where the cop's bullet had burst through | you wanted to run away
but you looked on | & now remember

FULL STOP, OR RATIONALIZING DEATH

Reminder: the sun is a star.

Stars explode.

Disclosure: I've forgiven myself for letting the cactus die.

Childcare and synchronous online classes are unsustainable.

One plus one remains two.

Hydrogen and oxygen is still water.

My books are never organized in any sort of order, always a struggle.

Dialectics contradict the wheel of life.

A tangible truth: the wooden chair nobody uses reminds me of Tatay.

NOSTALGIA

*fragments of memory and forgetfulness, gestures that are
rediscovered without ever having been learned, words that come
back, memories of lullabies*
    —Georges Perec

you say, is the painful longing
to return, so you spend nights rummaging

through drawers of memory—
old, new, passed on, found—

to create a past that doesn't exist.
What you mainly recall

is pain—admit it, not even the longing.
But in nights like tonight,

moonless, you long for the homecoming
shrill of cicadas, returning

from more than a decade
of painless sleep. Buried

in a Sally Ann trove
of memories, you wonder

why pain exists
even in a past someone

else created. Your daughter
remembers making a dollhouse

with the balikbayan box that belonged
to your mother, who mainly existed in voice

tapes and postcards, returning
you to a sandy cove in Zambales

that exists only in your memory. Reunited,
you relearn how to be an obedient son,

like when she once taught you
how to memorize

the multiplication table and do long
division. Say, you cannot return—

the cove is now buried
in lahar. Trying to make sense

of lost things,
you continue to draft

the eventual return
to a home that never was,

but the verses
you create lead nowhere. The long hours

spent thumbing through
sheaves of papers simply pile up. You memorialize

in a losing attempt to defy
extinction, resurrected

in verse. There is a task
you have not fulfilled—to forget

the pain of being
left behind,

the incessant need
to create

refuge,
a catacomb

where you could return
to light candles, a handful of soil

in which to plant
pain, grow it

into a pot of alyssum,
something small and simple,

to create a leafy garden
where cicadas could return.

THREE TANKA, WITH FATHER-IN-LAW

i

up on Hikosan
Yoshiaki and I share
a bowl of mountain
vegetable soup—Tengu's long
nose hovering above us

ii

driving down Kyushu
highways, Yoshiaki
slides a Bill Evans
CD and hums "Danny Boy"—
his daughter's favourite tune

iii

Yoshiaki's fish-
shaped nambu furin cling-clangs
outside my window
echoing in East Van wind
dancing with red maple leaves

SEPTEMBER, 1st PANDEMIC YEAR

Forgetting is akin
to remembering—

a colourless fedora,
faceless friends, bodies

without sinews, barely
shadows. I understand

why things are greener
here. I will not explain—

let you feel
instead, the longing

for something almost
felt. At the tip

of your amygdala—
a waft of fresh ground

coffee, dissolving
conversations, cadences

scribbled on the back
of receipts, fissured cups.

PASTICHE AFTER C.P. CAVAFY

As you book a ticket for Manila,
hope your flight has no delays.
Full of comfort in Business Class, sleep.
Bakunawa, Kapre,
a hungry Aswang—don't be afraid of them.
You have forgotten them anyway.
As long as you stay focused on your dream vacation,
as long as travel gives pleasure and adventure,
stirs your body from boredom.
Bakunawa, Kapre,
wild Aswang—you won't encounter them
unless you rewatch the *Shake, Rattle & Roll* franchise,
unless you remember the stories of your grandmother.

Hope your flight has no delays.
May there be many Summer Sales when,
hunting for bargains,
you enter airports you're seeing for the first time;
may you stop at Duty Free
to buy overpriced things,
electronic gadgets and magnets, whiskey and cigarettes,
tax-free perfume of every kind—
as many tax-free perfumes as you can.
And may you visit many North American suburbs
to shop and go on shopping from their malls.

Keep Manila always in your mind.
Vacationing there is what you work for,
but don't hurry the flight at all.

Better if it lays over somewhere,
so you have extra luggage by the time you reach the islands,
bourgeois with all the property you've accumulated,
not expecting Manila to make you rich.

Manila gave you heartaches.
Without her you wouldn't have migrated.
She's got nothing to give you now.

And you will find her plundered;
accredited as you have become, with a wall of diplomas,
you may have learned by then what these Manilas mean.

GRIEF

Late for a graveyard shift, I forget my keys and wonder why
    leaving home feels like grief.
Lost the rhythms to remember shopping lists, the newsprint
    songbook of grief.

Where are the mango trees that shade my childhood alleys
    and streets?
I sleepwalk through a scaffold city, lost in its gentrified grief.

Caesuras of migration aren't pauses but ruptures.
Midnight nostalgia is a black ice road towards grief.

With neither warmth nor recall, my tongue contorts in constant
    search for ways to speak, numbed by bus stop
advertisements on diasporic grief—

#howfardoyoutravel? In a box under my bed, I entomb epistolary
    voice tapes and handwritten dreams, recited like hymns
in despedidas where we drown collective grief.

Take pandesal as baon for your departure, bring me green
    grass as homecoming gift.
The fragments of ourselves, pieced together by grief.

PAPURI

Praise the bread.
    —Martin Espada

Praise the hospital worker clad
in white armour, mask and face shield,
breathing life despite knee-bending
exhaustion, poor wages. Praise
the housekeeper, steering her cart
through congested rooms and hallways
with the skill of a jeepney driver
singing Top 10s in deadened air. Praise
to the proof that greatness
is faceless. Praise the jeepney
drivers. Praise the peasants
who till land during dead season,
and the labourers for roads
under our feet. The high noon
for lunch of steamed rice
and dried fish. A drizzle, torrential
downpour, cyclone—rain
will pass. Praise the silver lining,
spotted from the minuscule window
of a seafarer, eight months aboard
an oil tanker, at home in open sea,
no one to talk to except for low-lying
clouds, elusive seabirds. Praise

the migrant worker, modern-day exile
blanketed with snowflakes or desert dust,
toiling past midnight with a worn-out
pair of rubber shoes. Praise also
the rubber shoes, gifted by a son to his mother,
purchased with his first paycheque
as a grape picker in wine valley. The sap
of loneliness and sacrifice. At night,
praise the stars and moon, sing
praise with the rhythm of a childhood tune.

III.   DAUNGAN

I do not know where else I belong.
—Ada Limón

DIE GARTENWELT, 1897

The garden world. Borderland poppies, warm
red and yellow petals, stems undulating, lithe

under the memory of frost. *Existing, I peer
and penetrate still* at spring, which I thought

would never arrive. But here, a proof that trust
between plants and sunlight is perennial. Pages

quiver like fragile insect wings, fluttering—
consistently surprising, emotionally resonant,

and well-crafted—words I keep with my shovel
and sprinkler tin can. Like the trimmed twigs

and leaves of a wind-flushed juniper
bonsai, these poems owe their foliage

to sharp pruning shears. On my palm—
a fleeting world, a garden in bloom.

A SELF IMMOLATION

In my desire to be Nude
I clothed myself in fire:—
Burned down my walls, my roof,
Burned all these down.
    —José Garcia Villa

My body did not feel
as my own. Windswept,
as though the river's
currents washed away
not to rejuvenate, but erase
layers of scars that allude
to loss and lullabies.
Prelude to wokeness,
a radical renewal sparked
in my desire to be Nude

exposed under the gaze
of a sky blazing like a pyre,
scorched to be in touch—
to touch and be touched.
To be in harmony with my skin,
nerves tight like string of a lyre,
I first let go of things thought
of as atavistically human
or insatiable hungers. Then,
I clothed myself in fire:—

tossed my hat and it drifted
like a phoenix, whose tail
ignited an underbrush. A wildfire
engulfed garments wrapped
around my body. I took refuge
in nakedness, barren proof
of beatings, and sought safety
in homelessness. With red fingertips
I set foundations aflame and
burned down my walls, my roof

—my words, I also
burned all these down.

THE GARDENER

Memory fades
like a summer dress,
you say, so you learn
to garden
in a corduroy jumpsuit—
sowing seeds
while sewing scenes,
dissipating like mist
on a daffodil's
folds. There's a collation
of dry roots and stems,
fans of fern
in a plot that your neighbour
abandoned—a bouquet
of colourful convenience,
the stuff that grows
itself. If no longer
remembering, then a rock—
perhaps you can be
a miner or a jeweller,
forever carving,
etching, revealing. Yet
the shed with a thousand
books has not a single
word on your favourite

daffodil dress,
folded in the drawer.

EXPECTATIONS

These are the old tasks.
      The calendar is only a guide.

Succour comes at night, candlelight
      an antidote to stygian

fog. Wait for a clearing, or else succumb
      to dark clouds. They mimic

despair, then dissipate. If you want, stay
      in your room. There's something to be opened

in every house besides doors. Open them—
      lean on the windowsill. Chet didn't jump.

Let me tell you a secret: Pandora is already out
      of surprises. No need to count

unfulfilled wishes. The moon repeats its cycles.
      You've heard them before.

CENTO: AN ANIMAL, A TREE, A DANCE

I can become
what I will,
he cried,
and grew

a tail. I wonder
what kind of animal
that makes me. Maybe

I'm some kind of
tree. Tell me,

does it hurt
the ground more
or the tree if
you are to extract it

by its roots? Perhaps
what I am is a dance
wandering

in search of bodies—
a stone, a leaf, a door.

KAMAYAN

The world begins at a kitchen table.
I eat therefore I am. The economy,

my teacher says, always means bread.
Hunger drives the search. Once,

I met a philosopher at a fiesta
for San Antonio de Padua, the patron

for finding lost things. We ate
pancit, lumpia, and grilled chicken

intestines. I told him I started smoking
to quit biting my nails. He said, words

from an empty stomach are ethereal. I said,
it's better to die with my stomach full

than empty, especially when plates are empty—
no matter what, we must eat to live.

AFTER A QUARREL

a smokescreen

           temporarily obfuscates

                      our vision

         as I keep alive

a crumbling incense

      sakura

               blossoms from Daiso

                  my hand is tempted

   to touch the flame

        to purge spaces

               of stains

the caving futon

      still emits heat

           like our flower bed

at dusk

   ushering a tsunami

          of memories

            littered

with debris   bodies

     bare   naked

         as a deck of dealt solitaire

you play as I pretend

      to dream

         by the windowsill

          because you hate walls

   & the midnight breeze

THE FLANEUR AS A BIRDWATCHER

Steady downpour, trailing cigarettes
caught in a sidewalk rivulet,

radiant in the criss-cross of headlights.
There's something about walking

that reveals quotidian birdlife: a crow
prances in the midst of homecoming

traffic to dine on urban roadkill,
a goose drools in a parking lot

craving a bygone pond
that it didn't inhabit in the first place,

a pigeon perches on the barbed wire
fence of a migrant welcome house,

and caffeinated lovebirds in glass cages
try hard to hide their blushing faces.

SWEAT LODGE
for Sam

In a forest clearing, he lays down
the foundation of a Sacred Fire,
while I, kneeling on thawing snow,
lift Grandfathers one by one
to the lodge's pit—
as if emptying myself of memories,
the deeper I get, the heavier.

SAY IT

Facing the bathroom mirror, say subservience.
It's subversive to tell the boss you're refusing

work on a Sunday. Even god has needs
to satisfy. Say, *I'm the Creator.* Minimum

wage earner, showing up on time for the rest
of the week, got a shoebox full of bills

for things you didn't want. There's no storage
in purgatory. Sixteen hours of toil without

overtime pay—two jobs (sometimes three).
One for the body, another for the debt

collector. Say, *Fuck it. I quit.* It sounds hollow
within bathroom walls. Say organize,

resist. Say capitalism is the disease and
a pill on the counter you swallow before daybreak.

ISOLATION

for Henry Doyle

sipping stale beer
listening to little

laughs loud
whispers   sinking
in a grey couch

grey is a mind in decay

Bukowski barks
isolation is the gift

isolation means deceased
a living dead

it's not the booze that kills but the loaded gun

if given isolation
take it
but don't keep it
get on your knees
                    offer it
                              to the gods

ON THE ROAD

The storks travel.
We drive. *To save energy,*

they gain altitude. I deflate

when she wants me to open
up. *Rising warm air*

on serpentine Sasaguri Pass.
Nehanzo always rests sideways.

Through prairies and quarries,
rocks roam as if sheep in pasture,
propelled towards things adrift—

thermal, temperamental.

As we move closer, we forget
we're also falling apart,

gliding in circles,
flightless kites.

ON STUDENT LOAN

in the orange dim of a salt lamp, you come
sudden as a gust of wind

a cool scalp caress in a forest
of academic texts—succinct & kinetic

you don't jargon, concrete as nouns
in writing workshops
where everyone seeks a payoff

you thrive on panic attacks & late submission

the amount received must be reciprocated—
paid in part, but never fully

no matter how hard I work, I am bound

to wither before you, exuding the same bloodless
vitality as the day I signed the contract
persevering

BORDERLINE BETWEEN—

sanity & insanity

inertia & movement

of cheeks & nose

pricked ingrown

blistered toes

Jack & Goose

gun & noose

peace & destruction

pills & sessions

peeled skin that feels not

perhaps too much

whiteness & hue

canvas & view

K & I

sea & sky

dream & life—

what & what?

HOMESICKNESS

On a bench dedicated
to Philippe, I light up
a cigarette. Cyclists swerve
to the yellowing lawn. I fan
the smoke with my hand,
wonder if it finds home
in clouds. Before rain,
I step on the stump
and walk to the pebble beach
crowded with crows. They caw
louder than gulls. From afar,
container ships appear
immobile. After living
like a goldfish in cupped hands,
a shoeless deckhand
leaps with his knapsack
into the bay and swims
his way back to his dead
mother. I wish I had
the courage to float.

IV.   LAKBAY

We came to transmit the shimmering
from which we came; to name it

we deal with a permanent voyage,
the becoming of that which itself had
become
—Etel Adnan

THE SUM OF ITS SALT

[1]

PROLOGUE

hold crocodiles
in veneration
& when uttering
any statement
witnessing it
in the water
cry out
in all subjection,
Nono,
Grandfather—
ask pleasantly
& tenderly
for safe passage
offer it
a portion
of the things you carry
in your boat—

[2]

it was said: *there was no old tree*
to which they did not attribute divine
honours & it was a sacrilege
to think of cutting it
even the very rocks, crags, reefs & points
along the seashore & rivers adored
an offering made on passing by
stopping there & placing the offering
upon the rock or reef

it was said: *the river of Manila*
had a rock that served
as an idol ~~of that wretched people~~
for many years & ~~its scandal~~
lasted ~~& it gave rise to many evils~~
~~until the fathers of St. Augustine~~
~~who were near there~~
~~broke it~~
~~& set up a cross~~

[3]

September, 2011

beneath lily-pad canopies
a saltwater crocodile   exhausted

     from three months of hiding
     is lured to the surface with a carcass

& lassoed out   of the wild
brackish currents of Agusan Marsh

     strangled   into submission   the savage
     suspected of haunting   a bucolic village

by feasting on carabaos   a breadwinner
& the head   of an innocent schoolgirl

     is then bequeathed with a dead
     hunter's name—Lolong

          The Guardian: *Imagine it in sepia*
          instead of rich full colour
          and this might be a photograph of a Victorian
          expedition team who have made it
          through miles of jungle
          into the Lost Valley of the Dinosaurs
          and bagged themselves
          an iguanodon.

[4]

A zoologist sedates and measures
        Lolong with two different methods

to ensure accuracy. *Until a crocodile*
        has been measured, he says, *we cannot claim*

to know its size. The Guinness
        World Records, expert arbiters

of fame, concludes he's the biggest beast
        in captivity—as McGee hypothesized

the tallest man resided in Patagonia—
        stealing the crown from an Australian

crocodile, Cassius—a name disowned
        by the boxing legend, Muhammad Ali.

[5]

hundreds flock from far-flung places to see / the untamed
ambassador in concrete enclosure / fresh asphalt backroads
unroll like carpet for tourists / who pay / twenty pesos to satisfy
curiosities / witness the body of a *living* / *fossil* / fenced / half-
submerged / in water / drained & replenished / too cold
for warm blood / stoned head basking / unmoved by shutters
for a fee / feel / his ancient skin / more sensitive than human
fingertips / nothing to fear / his snout / steel-roped
to educate—*the natural web of life* / *between predators & prey*

[6]

        it's not surprising

                he stretches

more than twenty-one

                        feet from the tip

      of his tail   to his snout

            & weighs more

than a ton

                    like a Cadillac

hearse—   the *Crocodylus porosus*

                      tows coffins

   a conduit

        that transports

                souls across

riparian forests & rivers

                to a field for the dead

[7]

Did the giant croc predict 7.6 quake?

—awakened

the imprisoned reptile

revels in underground

tremors   earthen rage

roaring from the epicentre

of resistance in Eastern Samar

through a fragmented

archipelago all the way

to Bunawan & thrashes

his tail at the bloodshot gaze

of caretakers & patrons

interpreting his refusal

as a prophetic warning—

earthquake, then tsunami

[8]

Lolong refuses
meals not
because he has
no appetite
and can last
months without
food: he is
on hunger strike.

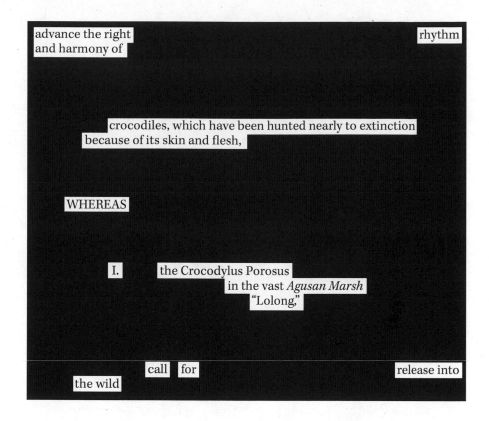

advance the right
and harmony of
rhythm

crocodiles, which have been hunted nearly to extinction
because of its skin and flesh,

WHEREAS

I.   the Crocodylus Porosus
in the vast *Agusan Marsh*
"Lolong,"

call   for
release into
the wild

FIFTEENTH CONGRESS OF THE REPUBLIC OF THE PHILIPPINES.
RESOLUTION DIRECTING THE PROPER SENATE COMMITTEE, TO
CONDUCT AN INQUIRY IN AID OF LEGISLATION, ON STRENGTHENING
AND AUGMENTING EXISTING LAWS PROTECTING VARIOUS
CROCODILE SPECIES IN THE COUNTRY.

[10]

necropsy (n.)

"post-mortem examination," 1839, from necro- "death, corpse" + opsis
"a sight"

    white bloated belly like the moon's refection on the pond

        bruised bowels

& heart

           abrasion of the skin in his head, teeth, claws
           pectoral & pelvic areas

    fungus

        mined mercury runoffs in blood

                no nylon cord residue

no shoes, human hair, hooves, or horns

    Perhaps it was love (fear) that killed Lolong?

        Web: *While Lolong may be gone, political pundits note that*
        his relatives—the human variety often clad in barong tagalog
        or a suit—still roam freely in the halls of the Philippine
        Congress, in reference to legislators being viewed as greedy
        for power and wealth. The Filipino street term for a greedy
        person is buwaya, which is also the local word for crocodile.

[11]

after Stéphane Mallarmé

harnessed by the Tree
    —of Life
    —his bones

suspended
to the ceiling—dissociated
    —from his hides

his innards
at home
    —in Bunawan

freezer-burned
    —in the afterlife

[12]

> *i ask them to*
>   *forgive me but*
> *all they see is*
>   *you*
>   —Juan Felipe Herrera

where to begin?
        let me first clarify
a few things   i have no need for rituals
                save
the chickens & pigs   spare me
from piety   let me return
            my beatified name
tears are precious—
each drop weighs more than the sum of its salt
                        i ask them to

keep the mourning
            for themselves
& the miseries of
            their own land
where children churn in perpetual departure
offer them   last
                rites
                at the harbour
                pray they learn to
                forgive me but

i will end the cycle here
i will carry them to their exiled futures
i will feed them my piece of the moon
i will wait at the opposite shore
    forbearing as a lighthouse
          in the briefness   of eclipse
i will be a guide   a glimpse
  of the horizon
      undulating until
        all they see is

              the vision
of repair   a people demanding
  repatriation—the gift
    of being
buried
in my mother's womb
      my fate cannot be undone
   it persists   in motion
    here w/
    you

[13]

EPILOGUE

But, of course, that infinite vision is an illusion, a god-trick.
—Donna Haraway

        trace blood-
   lines
             to an estuarine
      reptile   build edifices
   cast
      from his form
           bead his fangs
   of death
to ward   off
     the living   enter
         a cosmology
   of relations   primordial
         fear & adoration
     ancestor & kin
       summoned
in reverie   benevolent
     spirit   of justice
      take my body / devour
   me whole
    surrendering
       my soul so it may pass
        through the arch

of rain

                transformed   into a god

        while the *souls*   *of the drowned*

                      remain at sea forever

NOTES & ACKNOWLEDGMENTS

The section epigraphs are from "A Blessing" by James Wright in *Above the River: the Complete Poetry and Selected Prose* (Wesleyan University, 1990), "Off-Island Chamorros" by Craig Santos Perez (*92NY150*), "Ancestors" by Ada Limón in *The Carrying* (Minneapolis: Milkweed Editions, 2021), and *Surge* by Etel Adnan (Nightboat Books, 2018).

"Form as a Living Thing": the italicized lines are from *Border and Rule: Global Migration, Capitalism and the Rise of Racist Nationalism* by Harsha Walia (Fernwood Publishing, 2021) and "Introduction: Feel Your Way" in *The Cultural Politics of Emotion* by Sara Ahmed (Routledge, 2004).

"Bones Are Seeds": the poem is inspired by the Filipino migrant Benson Flores, who settled with a Filipino community on Bowen Island in the late 1800s. The title comes from the Filipino homonym *buto*, which means *bone* and *seed*. The phrase "man without love, country or soul" comes from "El Canto del Viajero" by José Rizal.

"Waking": the italicized lines are from *Notebooks, 1942–1951* by Albert Camus translated by Justin O'Brien (Marlowe & Company, 1994).

"Meditations": the part on cedar bark weaving is inspired by a workshop given by Karla Point.

"Extinctions": italicized line is from the lyrics of "My Way" written by Paul Anka.

"Pluvial: A Parking Lot Pastoral": written after *Pluviophile* by Yusuf Saadi (Nightwood Editions, 2020).

"When the Heart Catches Cold": the title comes from the Japanese, kokoro no kaze, or "a cold of the heart," a mental health campaign catchphrase from the 1990s. The phrase "full moon and bright stars" comes from J.P Seaton's translation of Li Po, *Bright Moon, White Clouds* (Penguin Random House, 2012).

"Suicide on Replay": refers to the novels *Footprints in the Snow* by Kenjiro Tokutomi, *Kokoro* by Sōseki Natsume, and *The Setting Sun* by Dazai Osamu.

"Ars Poetica": the italicized lines are from José Martí, as popularized by Ernesto "Che" Guevara in "Message to the Tricontinental," and from "Like You" by Roque Dalton, translated by Jack Hirschman in *Poemas Clandestinos Clandestine Poems* (Solidarity Publications, 1984).

"A Brief History of Walls": the italicized lines are from "Looking Around" by Charles Wright, while the title is after his book *A Short History of the Shadow: Poems* (Farrar, Straus, and Giroux, 2003).

"Locked Down": "left in the mountain to play with the pebbles of the stream" is from "Visiting the Hsi-Lin Temple" by Po Chü-i, translated by Arthur Waley.

"A Note": written after "A Note" by Wisława Szymborska, translated by Stanislaw Baranczak and Clare Cavanagh (*The New Yorker*, November 28, 2005).

"Basue": inspired by the Japanese term *basue*, as defined and articulated in the essay "Migrant Intimacies: Mobilities-in-Difference and *Basue* Tactics in Queer Asian Diasporas" by Dai Kojima (*Anthropologica*, Vol. 56 No.1, 2014).

"Autobiography: Manila": written after "Autobiography: New York" by Charles Reznikoff in *1937–1975, Volume II of The Complete Poems of Charles Reznikoff*, edited by Seamus Cooney (Black Sparrow Press, 1977).

"Filial Affairs": written after the book *asking myself, answering myself* by Shimpei Kusano (New Directions, 1984), the poem "Bone" by Nakahara Chūya, translated by Paul Mackintosh and Maki Sugiyama in *The Poems of Nakahara Chūya* (Gracewing, 2017), and *The Chieko Poems* by Takamura Kōtarō, translated by John G. Peters (Green Integer, 2007).

"High Junctions": the phrase "what work is" is from Philip Levine (*What Work Is*, Knopf, 1992).

"Nostalgia": the epigraph is from *Ellis Island* by Georges Perec, translated by Harry Mathews (New Directions, 2021). The poem is also inspired by the idea that nostalgia is an "unappeased yearning to return" in *Ignorance* by Milan Kundera, translated from French by Linda Asher (Harper Perennial, 2003).

"Pastiche after C. P. Cavafy": written after "Ithaca" by C. P. Cavafy, translated by Edmund Keeley in *C. P. Cavafy: Collected Poems* (Princeton University, 1975).

"Papuri": the epigraph is from "Alabanza: In Praise of Local 100" by Martín Espada in *Alabanza: New and Selected Poems 1982–2002* (W. W. Norton and Company Inc., 2004). The poem is rendered from my Filipino poem of the same title: Papuri sa mga nars at doktor/na balot ng puting baluti,/maskara at salamin. Patuloy/ang pagsagip ng buhay sa kabila/ng kakarampot na sahod/at ngatog-tuhod na pagod. Papuri/sa porter na parang drayber/ng dyip sa pagmaniobra ng istretser/sa makipot at pasikot-sikot na pasilyo./Papuri sa mga patunay na dukha/ang mukha ng kabayanihan. Papuri sa dyip./Papuri sa magsasakang nagbubungkal/ng lupa at sa manggagawang pinagpala/ng buhangin o piko ng aspalto. Papuri/sa tanghalian, baon na danggit at kanin/na binalot sa plastik. Papuri sa tirik na araw/na humuhubog sa mga butil ng bigas/at pawis.

Papuri sa tubig na pumapawi/ng uhaw at singaw ng lansangan./Katatapos lang ng ambon, ulan, o bagyo—/papuri sa balangaw na tanaw/mula sa kapirasong bintana ng marino,/walong buwan nang nasa laot/walang kausap kundi nagdaraan na ulap/at mailap na ibong-dagat. Papuri sa migrante/na puspusang naghahanap-buhay/abutin man ng gabi, mga makabagong destiyero/suklob ng niyebe o desyerto,/ suot ang pudpod na sapatos. Kaya't papuri rin/sa sapatos na regalo ng anak sa kaniyang ina/ gamit ang unang sweldo bilang tigapitas/ng ubas sa isang banyagang lambak/katas ng sakripisyo at pangungulila. Sa gabi,/pagpikit ng mga mata, papuri sa buwan at bituin./Papuri sa kabila ng dilim.

"Die Gartenwelt, 1897": written as a contribution to "House Anstruther Community Testimonial" by Shane Neilson (*Hamilton Arts & Letters*, Issue 15.1, 2022), and also a response to the cover of my chapbook, *Borderlands* (Anstruther Press, 2020), designed by Erica Smith. The phrase *"consistently surprising, emotionally resonant, and well crafted"* is from Jim Johnstone's comment on my manuscript. The line "Existing, I peer and penetrate still" is from "To the Garden, The World" by Walt Whitman.

"A Self Immolation": the epigraph is from "Lyrics: I" by José Garcia Villa in *Doveglion: Collected Poems* (Penguin Random House, 2008).

"Expectations": the italicized lines are from "A Poem Beginning with a Line by Pindar" by Robert Duncan in *The Opening of the Field* (New Directions, 1960).

"Cento: An Animal, a Tree, a Dance": uses lines from *Straw for the Fire: From the Notebooks of Theodore Roethke 1943–1962* by Theodore Roethke (University of Washington Press, 1980), *Body Count* by Kyla Jamieson (Nightwood Editions, 2020), *Pebble Swing* by Isabella Wang (Nightwood Editions, 2021), *The Flayed City* by Hari Alluri (Kaya Press, 2017), and *A Stone, A Leaf, A Door* by Thomas Wolfe (Scribner, 1945)

"Kamayan": italicized lines are from "Perhaps the World Ends Here" by Joy Harjo (*The Woman Who Fell from the Sky*, W.W. Norton and Company Inc., 1994).

"Say It": italicized lines are from "Pre-existing Conditions" by Steffi Tad-y in *From the Shoreline* (Gordon Hill Press, 2022).

"Isolation": "isolation is the gift" is from "Roll the Dice" by Charles Bukowski in *What Matters Most Is How Well You Walk Through the Fire* (Ecco, 2002).

"On the Road": italicized lines are found in the article "Image of the Day: Migrating Storks" by Jim Daley (*The Scientist*, May 25, 2018).

"Borderline Between—": the first and last lines are from the film *Girl, interrupted* (1999), directed by James Mangold and based on the book of the same title by Susanna Kaysen.

"The Sum of Its Salt": Parts 1 and 2 are found in *The Philippine Islands, 1493–1898*, a 55-volume book by Emma Helen Blair and James Alexander Robertson that consists of primary source documents for Philippine history translated into English.

Part 3: uses found text from "A captured beast that reminds us of a remote past" by Jonathan Jones (*The Guardian*, September 9, 2011).

Part 4: italicized lines are from the comments section in "Accurate length measurement for Lolong" by Adam Britton (*Croc Blog*, November 12, 2011).

Part 5: uses found words and phrases from "Bunawan mayor presents Lolong's Guinness World Record certificate to DENR" (*Government of the Philippines Official Gazette*, June 30, 2012), and from "Lolong never should have been captured" by Dr. Angel Alcala (*Rappler*, March 10, 2013).

Part 7: the italicized line is from a headline by ABS-CBN News (September 3, 2012).

Part 9: uses a document from the Senate of the Philippines Digital Archives.

Part 10: the etymology of "necropsy" is from *Etymology Online*. The italicized lines are from "What really killed Lolong?" by Adam Britton (*Croc Blog*, May 13, 2023) and "Philippines Sheds Crocodile Tears for Lolong, the World's Largest Reptile in Captivity" by Vittorio Hernandez (*International Business Times*, February 11, 2013).

Part 11: written after *A Tomb for Anatole* by Stéphane Mallarmé, translated by Paul Auster (North Point Press, 1983).

Part 12: the quatrain by Juan Felipe Herrera is from "Interview w/a Border Machine" in *Every Day We Get More Illegal* (City Lights Publishers, 2020).

Part 13: the epigraph is from the essay "The Persistence of Vision" by Donna Haraway. The italicized lines are from *The Philippine Islands*, translated from Spanish by Emma Helen Blair and James Alexander Robertson.

I also consulted "A Cultural History of Crocodiles in the Philippines: Towards a New Pact?" by Jan Van Der Ploeg et al. (*Environment and History*, Vol. 17 No. 2, May 2011).

*

Maraming salamat to my family—Kaori, Lorena Rin, Andres Haruto, ate Juvy, ate May, ate Bing, and Nanay—for the love, joy, and support.

Salamat to the Brick Books editorial collective and publisher, Alayna Munce, for trusting my poetry. To Cara-Lyn Morgan for her insights and keen editing.

Salamat to the writers, artists, and instructors who have encouraged, taught, and guided me throughout this journey: Kevin Chong, Itrath Syed, Amber Dawn, Steffi Tad-y, Karla Lenina Comanda, Chris Nasaire, Dr. Dennis Gupa, Hari Alluri, Fidel Rillo Jr., Fiona Tinwei Lam, Kyla Jamieson, Kevin Spenst, Henry Doyle, Sheryda Warrener, Ian Williams, Jong Yun Won, Jill Goldberg and Langara College's Stranger on the Train reading series, Brad Hyde from Pearson Adult Learning Centre, and my peers at the UBC creative writing workshops.

Salamat to poets Jen Currin, Wayde Compton, Ed Bok Lee, and Adrian De Leon for reading the collection and writing beautiful blurbs.

Isang bagsak sa mga kasama.

Salamat to the workers at public libraries and independent bookstores.

Thank you to the staff and jurors at BC Arts Council and Canada Council for the Arts for believing in my words and granting my work some financial support.

Gratitude to the Anstruther Press editorial collective for publishing *Borderlands* (2020), and to the staff, writers, editors, and artists of magazines, journals, and platforms where versions of my poems have appeared, including *The Fiddlehead, EVENT, CV2, Vallum The Temz Review, Tayo, Ricepaper,* and the play *buto/buto: bones are seeds,* produced by NPC3 and SEACHS.

To my departed loves: Tatay, Lola Alice, Mamay, brother Julius, Tito Boy, and cousin King. This book is for you, too.

To you, reader, maraming salamat.

Marc Perez is a poet and writer. Born and raised in Manila, he lives with his wife and two children in the unceded territories of the Musqueam, Squamish, and Tsleil-Waututh nations. *Dayo* is his first poetry collection.

Printed by Imprimerie Gauvin
Gatineau, Québec

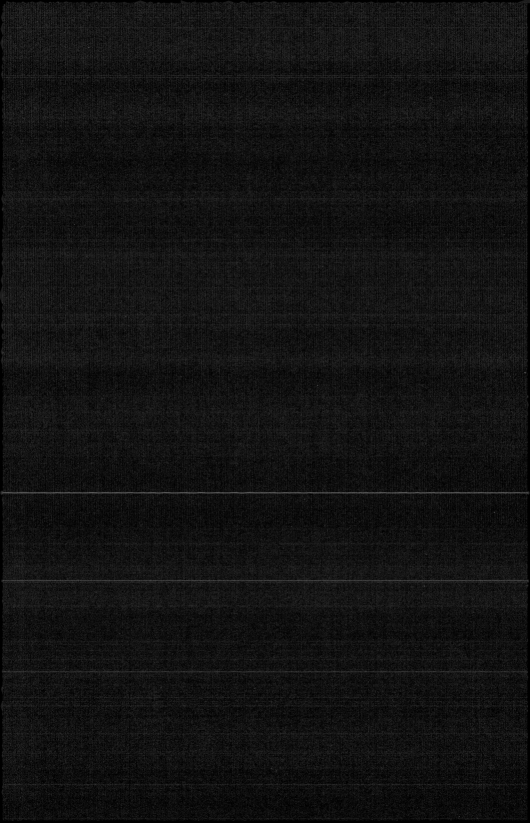